IMAGES OF LONDON

FULHAM

THE BROADWAY WALHAM GREEN

IMAGES OF LONDON

FULHAM

PATRICK LOOBEY

The
History
Press

Frontispiece: The Broadway, Walham Green, *c.* 1926.

First published in 2004 by Tempus Publishing Limited

Reprinted in 2010 by
The History Press
The Mill, Brimscombe Port,
Stroud, Gloucestershire, GL5 2QG
www.thehistorypress.co.uk

Reprinted 2013

British Library Cataloguing in Publication Data.
A catalogue record for this book is available from the British Library.

ISBN 978 0 7524 3231 1

Typesetting and origination by Tempus Publishing Limited.
Printed and bound in Great Britain.

Contents

The Greyhound public house, Fulham Palace Road, *c.* 1906.

The Author & Local History Sources

Born in 1947, Patrick Loobey has lived in Balham, Putney, Southfields, Wandsworth and Streatham, all within the Borough of Wandsworth. He joined the Wandsworth Historical Society (founded in 1953) in 1969 and has served on its archaeological, publishing and management committees, serving as chairman from 1991 to 1994 and 1998 to 2001. Having collected Edwardian postcards and photographs of Wandsworth Borough and the surrounding areas for almost thirty years, he has a wide-ranging collection encompassing many local roads and subjects.

This book complements other recent books by Patrick covering south-west London and surrounding areas: *Streatham*; *Battersea and Clapham*; *Balham and Tooting*; *Chelsea*; *Wandsworth*; *Wandsworth and Battersea at War*; *Putney and Roehampton*; *Putney: Past & Present*; and *Hammersmith & Fulham: Past & Present*.

The captions to the photographs in this book are but a brief glimpse into the varied and complex history of the area. For those seeking further information, the Fulham and Hammersmith Historical Society produce a series of booklets on aspects of local history and organise lectures and local history walks. They can be contacted via Keith Whitehouse. Tel: 020 7385 3723.

A vast collection of history resources are kept at: Hammersmith and Fulham History Centre and Local History Library, The Lilla Huset, 191 Talgarth Road, W6. Tel: 020 8741 5159. The staff are most helpful with any enquiries but an appointment should be made.

The photographs in this book are all from the author's collection of over 30,000 views of south-west and west London. Copies are available from Patrick Loobey, 231 Mitcham Lane, Streatham, London, SW16 6PY.

Introduction

The photographs in this book will give readers a glimpse back to when the housing development had just got started in Fulham and former market gardens and orchards were bought up as building plots. Fulham was renowned for its rich and fertile soil, producing fruit and vegetables for the London markets. The agricultural workers crowded around the small hamlets that grew up alongside these fields as at Crabtree, where wharves were added to take in hops for beer production and also at Broomhouse, first mentioned in the fifteenth century. Walham Green was to grow from the eighteenth century, but really expanded at the end of the nineteenth century as housing developments grew ever-northwards away from the river Thames and the arrival of the underground railway in 1880.

The heart of Fulham was near the parish church of All Saints, where the Bishops of London had their London palace for over 400 years and had owned the Manor of Fulham since the eighth century. Putney Bridge, opened in 1729, was a spur to the growth of the village, and the number of inns and alehouses, for instance, increased to supply the needs of passing travellers. Large riverside mansions were built in the seventeenth and eighteenth centuries as city gents built up their riches and moved to country estates; Brandenburgh, Hurlingham, Peterborough and Broomwood Houses were among the largest. Most have now been swallowed up for housing projects, but Hurlingham survives as a sports club.

As the population grew during the nineteenth century, more facilities had to be built to accommodate their requirements; schools, libraries, hospitals, fire stations, churches and street lighting were added to the street scene. Farriers, grocers, bakers, and house furnishers arrived, along with tradesmen such as gas fitters, plumbers, painters, decorators and an extraordinary number of shoe and boot repairers.

Fulham parochial council had already built the town hall at Walham Green in 1890, ready for the formation of the London Boroughs in 1899. An early decision was to build Fulham's own electrical power station at Townmead Road, powered by burning refuse. The political scene soon altered when party affiliations became the means of getting some action on social issues. The Borough of Fulham was amalgamated with Hammersmith in 1965 to form a new enlarged entity, the London Borough of Hammersmith and Fulham, and the town hall in Walham Green was relegated to minor functions.

Bus services increased in frequency to serve the quest for goods at the new shopping districts of North End Road, Wandsworth Bridge Road and in many other thoroughfares, while also providing the means of seeking work outside Fulham. The railway companies had largely bypassed Fulham; any main lines were on the outskirts of the borough and Fulham did not have any railway viaducts or embankment cuttings through the housing stock.

The underground railways have served the area well since 1874, with lines leading to Hammersmith, Wimbledon and the West End. The only fly in the ointment was the renaming of the stations: North End, Fulham was only renamed West Kensington to suit the developers, William Henry Gibbs and John P. Flew, who had built 1,200 houses in North End and wanted the area to be an extension of Kensington. Walham Green was renamed Fulham Broadway, partly to suit the local shopkeepers but also the councillors who felt the town name of Fulham was not featured on any of the stations.

Trams only worked the section along Fulham Palace Road, as the road network was too narrow to accommodate a tramway system in the rest of Fulham.

Forms of entertainment were brought in with the Granville Theatre at Walham Green and the Grand Theatre at the foot of Putney Bridge. The area was well served by cinemas, Walham Green and North End Road having nine in all. Two other cinemas served the rest of Fulham, but, with the advent of television in the 1950s, they gradually closed.

Industry was mainly confined to the Thames riverside. Formerly the haunts of osier gatherers and often flooded, the land proved useful for firms needing a riverside wharf in the nineteenth century, such as sugar manufacturers. The Imperial Gas Works, Manbré & Garton, Kop's Brewery by Wandsworth Bridge and Van der Bergh's margarine factory were a few of the large firms by the river.

As the industrial areas became derelict in the 1970s and 1980s, the land was used by developers for residential flats overlooking the Thames. A supermarket has been built on the riverside along Townmead Road but there are few in Fulham, the older-style Victorian outlets being suitable to adaptation for modern requirements.

Patrick Loobey

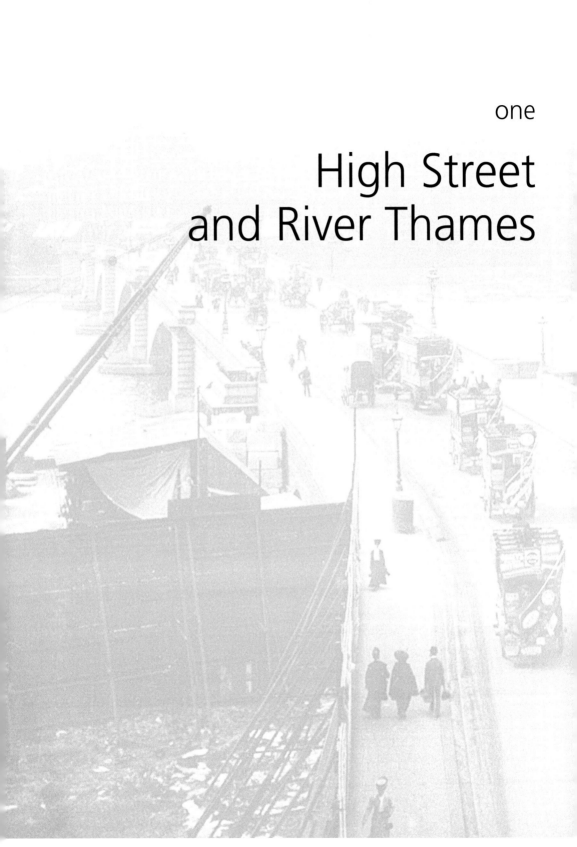

one

High Street
and River Thames

Putney Bridge, *c*. 1885. To the right is Putney Bridge, built in 1727, the first to be built between London Bridge and Kingston and managed by the Fulham Bridge Co., which collected tolls from those wishing to cross. The timber structure, which quickly became known as Putney rather than Fulham Bridge, was in constant need of repair due to the sinking of the piles and damage from floating ice and errant barges. The rights of the company were bought out by the Metropolitan Board of Works and the bridge freed of tolls on Saturday 26 June 1880. To the left is the Chelsea Waterworks Co. aqueduct built in about 1854 and taken for the site of the present bridge opened in 1886.

The Fulham Toll House on Putney Bridge, with the toll collector about to collect his last payment in 1880 just as the tolls were abolished.

The Fulham Toll House and Putney Bridge in 1878. The bridge was very narrow and was proving an impediment to road and river traffic, so the Metropolitan Board of Works decided to rebuild, which was undertaken between 1884 and 1886.

Putney Bridge, *c.* 1906. The bridge was designed by Sir Joseph and Mr Edward Bazalgette, both renowned for their work on the Thames Embankment and the installation of London's sewerage system. The bridge was opened on Saturday 29 May 1886 by the Prince of Wales, later King Edward VII. The bridge was widened from 44ft to 77ft between 1931 and 1933 to accommodate the ever-increasing volumes of traffic.

The wharf at Fulham and Putney Bridge, *c.* 1900. A Thames sailing barge is docked at Swan Wharf. Alongside are some oast houses engaged in the brewing trade and the coal wharf of Cramer Roberts. A sheltered housing scheme called Swan Court was built on the site in the 1980s. In the background is All Saints parish church.

Broomhouse Dock, *c.* 1900. The dock is the last remnants of the ferry to The Feathers Inn at Wandsworth. The area had its own small hamlet right up to the seventeenth century when twelve inhabitants were recorded as paying rates in 1605. The dock walls have been refaced in brick and concrete and the gravel foreshore has been replaced with a bed of concrete. The dock now has a gated entrance from Broomhouse Lane.

Aerial photograph of Fulham, *c.* 1926. The grounds of the Bishop's Palace are to the top left, with Putney Bridge and the railway bridge to the left. Hurlingham Park is at the bottom right and the large mansion blocks of Hurlingham Court have yet to be built on the riverside.

Putney Bridge and Fulham, *c.* 1926. The parish church lies at the centre, with Swan Wharf, bought by Fulham Council in 1900, in use for discharging rubbish into waiting barges.

Rivermead Court from the railway bridge, *c.* 1935. To the left is Hurlingham Court, Ranelagh Gardens. The large residential Rivermead Court Estate was built in 1929-1930 by the Prudential Assurance Co. to the designs of the architects Messrs Joseph of London. The three blocks contain 211 flats but do not have a No.13, 113 or 213 out of superstition. A few extra flats have been provided for management staff.

The Grand Theatre, on the corner of the High Street and Putney Bridge Approach, *c.* 1926. The theatre was built in 1897 to the designs of W.G.R. Sprague, with a seating capacity for 2,239 patrons. This was reduced in 1914 to 1,411 seats. Frequently used as a cinema, the theatre was demolished in 1957-1958 and replaced by an office block. On the left is the King's Arms public house, an old coaching inn first recorded in the early sixteenth century but rebuilt in 1888. The pub lay derelict throughout the 1990s but has been refurbished and now bears the name The Larrik.

Fulham House, High Street, *c.* 1912. Dating from about 1740, Fulham House saw use as a
school throughout the major part of the nineteenth century until 1879, when local builder
Parkins Hammond Jones bought it. From 1904 the War Office used it as a Territorial
Army Headquarters, the 25th London Cyclist's Battalion taking up residence here. The
front garden was built over during the Second World War but a local conservation group
managed to get this demolished in the 1980s and the house has been restored and is now
one of the architectural gems of Fulham.

Putney Bridge Station, *c.* 1910. The Metropolitan Railway Co. opened this station in 1880
as Putney Bridge and Fulham Station. The line was extended to reach Wimbledon with
the construction in 1889 of the Thames Railway Bridge, downstream of Putney Bridge. By
1902, as the Hurlingham Club became a fashionable venue, the name was altered to Putney
Bridge and Hurlingham Station, as in this view. The present name of Putney Bridge Station
was finalised in 1932.

High Street, Fulham, *c.* 1914. The High Street was first mentioned in 1391 as Burystrete, a Saxon term for lying within the defensive earthworks of Fulham Palace. This was the centre of Fulham's village. The High Street was widened in 1906 to accommodate the London County Council (LCC) electric tramway system and only on the east side do any buildings date from before this time. Two buildings to note are the Golden Lion public house at No.53, dating from 1836, and the Fulham National School, now the Fulham Preparatory School, at No.47a, built in 1861.

High Street Fulham, west side, *c.* 1939. The older shops remaining after the road widening in 1906 were finally demolished in the late 1920s and replaced by Parkview Court flats and ground-floor shops in 1932.

Above: The High Street from Fulham Road, *c.* 1900. To the right is the Kings Head public house. First mentioned in 1695 it was rebuilt in 1884 but was only to last until the road widening in 1906 to accommodate the LCC trams. The rest of the western parade of shops, some dating from the seventeenth and eighteenth centuries, was demolished in the late 1920s.

Right: The King's Head public house, High Street, *c.* 1915. The reason for the 1905-1906 rebuilding of the pub is evident by the tram trolley pole to the left of the building. The three-storey, three-bay extension at the far end was found to be unstable and was demolished in the 1970s/1980s and now forms a small garden attached to the pub.

Bishop's Park, *c.* 1905. The grounds for the park were originally part of the Bishop of London's Palace at Fulham. What had been the Bishop's Meadow was transferred to the Fulham District Board of Works in 1884 for use as a recreation ground. A further land grant of the West Meadow was added in 1889 but it was not until the river wall was finished in 1893 that the park was officially opened.

The Avenue and moat, Bishop's Park, *c.* 1912. The moat surrounding the palace was first mentioned in documents in 1392 but local tradition has associated it with the Viking incursion in AD 800-801. Archaeological excavation has uncovered even earlier remains dating from pre-Roman times, indicating that it was an enclosure around an early settlement. The Neolithic (*c.* 3,000 BC) and Roman periods are evident from the remains which are on display in the museum of Fulham Palace. The moat, once filled with water from the Thames, was filled in from 1921 onwards as a sanitary measure, but can still be traced alongside the Avenue, in Moat Gardens and in Victorian maps.

Bishop's Park, *c.* 1907. The ornamental nature of the flowerbeds and ornaments such as the drinking fountain were more important during the late Victorian and Edwardian era, as seen here with two park keepers posing for the camera.

The Bowls Club, Bishop's Park, 1926. Some serious deliberation is taking place among the officials at this bowls match. The park has been provided with areas set aside for tennis, cricket, bowls and a putting course. A roller-skating area has been set aside and street hockey is also now played in the park.

Rigault Road, *c.* 1914. The road name was approved for use in 1897 but planning applications had been submitted between 1894 and 1896. In 1855 the government purchased the former Burlington Academy in Burlington Road for the construction of a women's refuge or prison. The prison was closed in 1888 and sold off in 1893 and the majority of the buildings subsequently demolished for housing development. What appears to be the prison laundry survives as the Burlington Lodge Studios on the corner of Rigault Road and Buer Road.

Fulham Park Gardens, *c.* 1913. The developer of the site of the former women's prison had applied for the road names to be acceptable; these were approved in 1897. The planning applications for the houses in this road were submitted between 1895 and 1899, a four-year building programme.

All Saints parish church, *c.* 1912. The church is first mentioned in 1154 but a church
has probably stood here since the late Saxon period, over a thousand years. The tower is
now the oldest standing structure in Hammersmith or Fulham, dating from 1440. The
parishioners of Fulham could not afford to build a new church in the 1870s and so brought
in the architect Sir Arthur Blomfield, born at Fulham Palace, to totally rebuild the body
of the church, saving the tower. Several Bishops of London are buried here. To the left is
Pryor's Bank Pavilion, named after a Gothic house built here in 1837 and demolished in
1897. The pavilion building was first used as refreshment rooms and now houses offices of
the council's parks and cemeteries department.

Bishop's Palace, *c.* 1913. The Manor of Fulham was granted to the Bishop of London in
AD 704, although the earliest record of a building on this site only dates from the early
eleventh century. The bishops used Fulham Palace as their country residence, their town
property being situated alongside St Paul's church in the city. The palace was enclosed
by a moat almost a mile in length. The building, dating from the fifteenth, sixteenth and
eighteenth centuries, had been the bishop's official residence from the eighteenth century
until leased to the borough council by the Church Commissioners in 1973.

William Powell Almshouses, Church Gate, *c*. 1913. The almshouses were built from a bequest by Sir William Powell on his death in 1680 to house twelve poor women of the parish. The almshouses were first erected in Burlington Road but were transferred to Church Gate in 1868–1869.

two

Fulham Palace Road

The LCC trams were introduced along Fulham Palace Road in 1909 and survived until the introduction of trolley buses in 1935. On the left is Moat Gardens, part of Bishop's Park, and to the right the houses were built on what was once called High Bank, an outer earthwork of the palace defences, and the houses in some instances are showing signs of subsidence.

Fulham Palace Road, *c.* 1914. The trolley poles and wires seemed to darken the sky right up to their removal in 1962. Of interest to house owners today, on the corner of Niton Street are the complete cast-iron railings on the low front walls that were removed for the wartime scrap drives during 1941 and 1942. Sadly some of the stone balls are missing from the house façades today.

St Etheldreda's church, Fulham Palace Road, *c.* 1913. Situated on Fulham Palace Road, between Gowan Avenue and Cloncurry Street, the church opened as a mission hall on 28 November 1896, this becoming the parish hall when the permanent church opened. Previously, from January 1885, services had been held in a laundry ironing room in Gowan Avenue and in a music room at 120 Gowan Avenue. A.H. Skipworth was the architect for the hall and the main church, whose foundation stones were laid on 16 June 1896 and 15 June 1898. As building work commenced, the church was consecrated on 2 April 1897, 25 June 1899 and finally on 26 June 1900. The church was bombed and destroyed on 29 September 1940. The foundation stone for the new church, consecrated on 18 October 1958, was laid on 15 October 1955. Guy Briscoe was the architect. Part of the parish of St Clement's was absorbed in 1968 to form the parish of St Etheldreda with St Clement.

Fulham Palace Road, *c.* 1914. Development of Fulham Palace Road was a long-term enterprise, with plans for houses at Nos 45 and 47 being submitted in 1871, those at 121 to 127 submitted in 1883 and those around the high 380s in 1895. The 1871 Ordnance Survey map still shows the orchards and fields of fruit and vegetables that Fulham had been renowned for, its rich soil supplying the London markets.

Fulham Palace Road and St Clement's church, top *c.* 1914 and lower *c.* 1906. The foundation stone for the mission church was laid on 31 October 1882 and it was opened on 22 February 1883. The architect, Arthur William Blomfield, also designed the main church whose foundation stone was laid 11 July 1885. The church was consecrated on 3 July 1886 and the mission hall then became the parish hall at 286 Fulham Place Road. The church closed in October 1964 and was demolished in late 1969. The parish was divided into three with one part designated to St Alban's, one part to St Paul's and the remaining third, which included the church, vicarage and hall, going to St Etheldreda's. The new church was opened on 11 March 1976 with Clifford Haigh House built on part of the previous church land.

The Greyhound public house, Fulham Palace Road, *c.* 1911. The Greyhound was built
in the 1890s and has recently been renamed as The Puzzle. Wills & Sons' corner general
store, with the zinc baths hanging outside, doubled up as a telegraph and post office. In the
distance is St Clement's church. The parade of shops opposite the pub, between Ellaline
Road and Nella Road, were built shortly after in 1913.

The Nurses Training Home, Fulham Palace Road, *c.* 1906. As the population of Fulham
increased and the resources of Fulham Hospital were in ever-increasing use, it became
necessary to attract good nursing staff. Accommodation had been provided by the use of
houses in St Dunstan's Road, but by the turn of the twentieth century it was deemed urgent
to build a nurses' home opposite the infirmary. Princess Christian, daughter of Queen
Victoria, opened Brandenburg House, erected at a cost of £12,839 for sixty nurses on 6 July
1905. An unusual feature was the provision of a tunnel under Fulham Palace Road for the
nurses to connect to the hospital opposite. By 1923 there were 110 nurses requiring housing
and a new nurses' home was opened in 1929. The house has since been sold to a private
company but the building still provides accommodation for students.

The Fulham Infirmary, from Fulham Palace Road, top *c.* 1913, and from St Dunstan's Road, lower *c.* 1915. The infirmary was opened in 1850 as the Fulham Union Workhouse. Additional wings were added in 1871 and in 1884 the new infirmary was opened. The title 'hospital' was only added in 1928. The War Office took it over from 1915 to 1919 for treating wounded soldiers, with it becoming Fulham Military Hospital. The old hospital was gradually demolished from 1966 onwards as the new Charing Cross Hospital moved here from central London. The seventeen-storey hospital, with 900 beds, was opened by Queen Elizabeth II on 22 May 1973. Approximately twenty-five yards of the original workhouse cast-iron railings and pillars survive along the Fulham Palace Road frontage.

Fulham Palace Road, *c.* 1913. Billy Berger & Son are promoting their 'antiseptic' shaving saloon on the awning above their outlet on the right. Averill Street is on the right at the end of this parade and Ellaline Road is on the left.

Fulham Palace Road, *c.* 1913. Yeldham Road on the left is on the northern border of Fulham parish, where it meets with Hammersmith parish. The pavements appear to be thronged with people busying along the road, as walking was the cheapest means of locomotion. For this reason the boot and shoe repairer was always in occupation, a trade that has almost disappeared today. Biscay Road is the next street on the left.

Fulham Palace Road, *c.* 1913. Biscay Road is on the right. The large building further along the road is part of the Guinness Trust Buildings, erected in 1901. Fulham Council has saved the ratepayers money by attaching the street lamps to the LCC tramway trolley poles.

The Rifle public house, 80 Fulham Palace Road, *c.* 1913. This late nineteenth-century public house on the corner of Distillery Lane was renamed the Golden Gloves for about forty years when the Mancini brothers, Toni and Alfred, and their father, all of boxing fame, managed the pub. The pub was renamed The Suffolk Punch in about 1996. On the next corner is the Distillers Arms public house, known locally as the Distillers, in Chancellors Road, which marks the boundary between Fulham and Hammersmith.

Beryl Road, *c.* 1914. The road name was approved in 1890. The drainage applications for the houses were applied for in 1891 and 1892.

Bowfell Road, *c.* 1912. The road name was approved in 1911 and in this scene dated about 1912, although the houses have been completed and a solitary street lamp erected, the road surface has not yet been finished or the pavements laid. The road name was not to appear in local guides until 1915.

Crabtree Lane, *c.* 1914. Before the First World War, the lane was still a gravel-surfaced track leading to the riverside. Until the 1890s, when the large factories of industry moved to the area alongside the Thames, the land hereabouts was mainly market gardens, with orchards and strawberry fields. A small hamlet had sprung up at the end of Crabtree Lane with the basket-weavers using the osier beds nearby. In the late eighteenth century Joseph Attersall became an early industrialist of Fulham; he had a business as a maltster in some oast houses at Crabtree and added a vitriol factory, chalk wharf and lime kilns.

The Crabtree public house, Rainville Road, *c.* 1903. As the small hamlet grew at Crabtree, a small inn called the Pot House was opened in the 1760s to fill the needs of the agricultural workers and basket-weavers. The pub was renamed, appropriately, the Three Jolly Gardeners but rebuilt in the late 1890s on a larger scale and renamed The Crabtree. Behind the pub, in this view, are the eighteenth-century oast houses on the riverside.

Ellaline Road, *c.* 1920. The road name was approved in 1911 and building applications were submitted in 1911 and 1912. A trade much in demand among these new houses would have been that of Harry Woodbridge, decorator at No.23 in 1914.

Finlay Street, *c.* 1920. The road name was approved in 1901. The only trade or employment listed for this road in 1912 and 1917 is that of Mr Alfred Leggett at No.6, a pianoforte tuner and teacher of violin, mandolin and banjo.

Gowan Avenue, *c.* 1913. The road name was approved in 1890 and house construction started in 1893. The road did not boast many tradesmen, as the only ones listed for 1917 are George Henry Elliot at No.44, a precious-stone cutter, and John Brown & Son at No.10, monumental sculptors. The road name has become world-famous as the scene of the tragic murder of thirty-seven-year-old Jill Dando, the BBC journalist and co-presenter of the BBC television programme *Crimewatch*, on the doorstep of her home at No.29 on 26 April 1999.

Gresswell Street, *c.* 1913. The road name was approved in 1901 and the houses built during 1905. In 1912, Alfred Blackall, plumber and decorator, lived at No.27. The only major listing for this road in 1917 was the fact that the LCC school appeared on the south side of the road.

Harbord Street, *c.* 1920. The road name was approved in 1901 and the houses built in 1904. Where any trades are listed in the directories for 1912, this would only indicate the business undertaken from those addresses. In 1912 there was at No.142 a Miss Gertrude Davis, dressmaker, and at No.33 James Charles, insurance agent.

Inglethorpe Street, *c.* 1913. The road name was approved in 1901. Building operations must have commenced soon after applications were submitted in 1903-1904 for the houses at 1 to 51 and 2 to 52. Stevenage Road is at the far end, with a stack of piping at a wharf waiting to be transported. On the left, at No.53 on the corner of Woodlawn Road, is Wills & Sons Oil and Color stores; it was common at the beginning of the twentieth century for these stores to use the American spelling for colour. They supplied household items, pots, pans, zinc baths, paraffin oil and the powders for colouring paint.

Kenyon Street, *c.* 1906-1907. The road name was approved in 1901 and building applications were submitted in 1903 for all of the houses from 1 to 53 and 2 to 56. In 1912 listed at No.58 is Richard Offer, stationer and newsagent, and at No.74 James V. Flanagan, builder and decorator. There are two horse-drawn and two hand-pushed delivery vehicles in this scene.

Lambrook Terrace, *c.* 1913. Although the road name was approved in 1890, it wasn't until 1898 that applications for building work were submitted to Fulham Council for Nos 1 to 39 and 2 to 40. The following year, 1899, saw applications for Nos 41 to 49 and 42 to 50 to be connected to the main drainage system. The houses are split into two, a ground floor and first floor. Several home trades are listed for 1912, with Mrs Stevens, costumer, at No.18, Louis Gray, music teacher, at 14a and two dressmakers, Miss Storch at 20 and Mrs Ireland at 34. At 38a was the Salvation Army quarters.

Larnach Road, *c.* 1925. The road name was approved in 1911, the same year all of the house drainage applications were served to the council. Mrs Annie Sewell, a teacher of music, is listed at No.34 in 1914.

Oxberry Avenue, *c.* 1913. The road name was approved in 1887. The only trade listed in 1917 and for many years was at No.58, being the offices of H. Windsor & Co., general contractors.

Parfrey Street, *c.* 1919. The road name was approved in 1902, with drainage applications served in 1903 and 1904. At the far end is the Pimlico Wheel Works in Rannoch Road. A small three-wheel dairy cart and a hand-pushed cart with a ladder are the only vehicles in the road. In 1914 there was at No.25a Charles Yates, a plumber, and at No.58 an O. Loler, sculptor.

Queensmill Road School, 3-11 Lysia Road, *c.* 1920. The school first opened as Macmurdo Road School and on renaming of the road it became Queensmill Road School on 10 May 1905. The new road name, Queensmill Road, was approved in 1900. In 1917 Mr G. Godley was headmaster, Miss H.J. Male headmistress and Miss E.M. Sanders the infant's mistress. The school was renamed as Queens Manor School on 1 September 1951. The school has 203 pupils, including those in the special needs unit.

St Dunstan's Road, upper, *c.* 1914 with Fulham Infirmary on the right, lower. *c.* 1906. The road name was approved in 1891. House construction occurred over an extended period as the first were planned for 1887, with the majority erected in 1889, and a few added in the 1890s and as late as 1906. In 1914 many trades were listed, including Cox, Bruton & Tongue, boiler composition manufacturers, at 51, Miss Constance Prowse, confectioner, at 54 and Charles Prowse, mason, at 54 and 56. Sometimes the person's name is reflected in their occupation, as there was an Alfred Toone, professor of music, at No.21 and Alfred Lines, painter, at No.130. In the earlier scene, on the left is the entrance to the Captain Maryatt School, now the William Morris Academy.

Rannoch Road, *c.* 1926. The road name was approved in 1902. The planning applications were submitted over a two-year period, 1 to 71 and 2 to 54 in 1911 and the rest in 1912. The small group of houses from 64 to 70 were added in 1913.

Silverton Road, *c.* 1926. The road name was approved in 1911 and all of the properties, from 1 to 37 and 2 to 38, had drainage applications filed that year.

Skelwith Road, *c.* 1926. The road name was approved in 1911 and drainage applications were submitted in the same year for Nos 1 to 30, with some additions made in 1912. Two occupations were listed for 1914: Alan Robertson Wells LSA Lond, physician and surgeon, at No.1, and, almost as important, a Miss Marion Tutty, midwife, at No.33. At the far end in Rainville Road, alongside the river Thames, is the factory of Bryce & Western, shirt manufacturers.

Winslow Road, *c.* 1914. The road name was approved in 1896 with the even-numbered houses built that year and the odd numbers in 1899. At sometime the road name was changed from Brandenburgh Road, formerly the site of Brandenburgh House on the waterside. This large house was first built in the seventeenth century but became famous in 1820 as the London home of Caroline of Brunswick, consort of the Prince Regent, later King George IV. At the far end is the large factory of Manbré & Garton Saccharine Co., glucose manufacturers. The firm moved here in 1874 and finally closed in 1986.

Yeldham Road, *c.* 1914. The road name was approved in 1880. On the left is Yeldham House viewed from Fulham Palace Road. House construction commenced in 1881 and 1882. The only firm based in the road was that of T.M. Fairclough & Sons, Carmen, in a yard next to No.59 in 1914. Mrs Church at No.45 and Mrs H. Singer at No.33 were both dressmakers and John Lewis Nicquet, decorator, lived at No.46.

Blakes' Wharves Ltd, Stevenage Road, *c.* 1932. The company specialised in packing and shipping containers across the world from their wharf at Fulham from before the First World War until the 1970s, when the wharves were demolished. During the 1930s, the company had a contract with the de Havilland aircraft company to pack into wooden containers many marks of complete aircraft for export all over the globe.

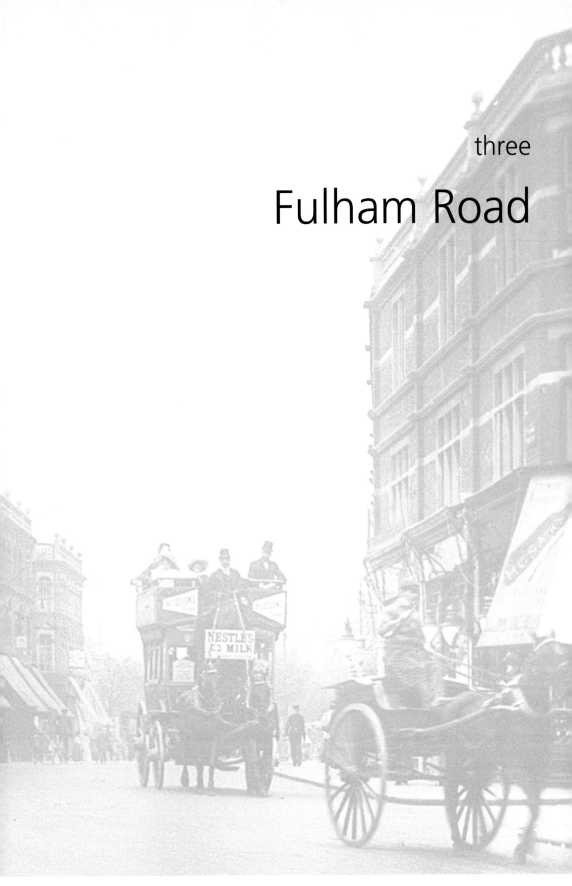

three

Fulham Road

Fulham Road, *c.* 1907. A horse-drawn bus is negotiating the roadway in Fulham Road opposite the Kings Head public house in the High Street. The petrol-engine bus was only just being introduced to the streets of London and was still considered a rare sight. The horse bus, which was gradually being phased out, survived until 1912.

Fulham Road, *c.* 1912-1913. A horse-drawn delivery vehicle from the London & North Western Railway Co. is stopped outside the parade of shops on the corner of Fulham Road and the High Street. The railway companies supplied a delivery service for bulky items from most of their stations. The drainage applications for this parade, Nos 947 to 961 Fulham Road, were submitted in 1897, the same year as Drive Mansions, alongside.

Drive Mansions, Fulham Road, *c.* 1913. This block of residential flats, opposite Waldemar Avenue, was built in 1897. The mansions were under the management of the Fulham & Hampstead Property Co. from their offices at flat No.105 in 1917. At the rear of the mansions space was set aside for the Drive Club and tennis courts. The shop at No.947 Fulham Road, alongside, is offering ice creams at 2d, 4d and 6d.

Fulham Road, *c.* 1914. In 1914 the parade of shops from Oxberry Avenue to Waldemar Avenue comprised Mrs Best's Drive Dress Agency at No.778, where second-hand clothes were bought and sold; George Kingston, butcher, at 776 has the blinds down to protect his window display; and Robert Turner's Furnishing and General Ironmongers store at 774 displays a large key above the premises to advertise his key-cutting service.

Fulham Road, with Munster Road on the left, c. 1913. The parade of shops on the left, Nos 861 to 875, were erected in about 1903. To the right and out of view is the Durrel Arms public house, recently renamed as just The Durrel.

Fulham Road, with Munster Road on the right, c. 1913. Frost & Co. stores, on the left, has a wonderful produce display on the pavement outside the premises. This busy shopping parade on the left, near Munster Road, still retains many of the glazed tile panels on the party walls separating the outlets.

Fulham Road, *c.* 1914. This section of Fulham Road, near Crookham Road and Rostrevor Road, had a variety of outlets including Hill and Tynne's dairy on the left and, on the corner of Rostrevor Road, Thomas Inch Ltd, physical culture expert. Almost every window of the premises right up to the roof is covered with the name Thomas Inch.

Fulham Road, *c.* 1926. Dancer Road is on the right. The oil and hardware store on the left has a display of zinc tubs hanging from the shop fascia and an arrangement of wooden ladders on the pavement outside. The display of goods for sale on the pavement would today be seen as an obstruction and frowned upon by most local authorities.

Fulham Road, *c.* 1930. Information from Chris Amies, who is compiling a list of Fulham and Hammersmith public houses, is that the off-licence at No.674, on the corner of Rostrevor Road, may have once been a small public house called the Malt and Hops.

Fulham Road, *c.* 1914. Rostrevor Road is on the left. The Munster Park Methodist chapel on the corner of Chesilton Road, which seated 1,000 worshippers, was opened on 29 March 1882. The foundation stone was laid on 28 June 1881; the architect was James Weir. The church roof suffered bomb damage on 16 November 1940 and the church was repaired and reopened on 25 March 1950. The church closed on 7 February 1971 and was demolished later that year. A smaller church using one of the previous halls was opened on 7 October 1972 but finally closed in September 1994. The site has been built on with a three/four-storey office block and shops.

Fulham Road, c. 1914. Munster Park Methodist chapel is to the left corner of Chesilton Road. The church was founded with the erection of an iron chapel in 1880 that remained in use until the permanent church opened. A schoolroom was built in 1882.

Fulham Road with Purcers Cross Road to the right, c. 1914. To assist the historian, the builders of the shopping parade, with living accommodation above, added the construction date of 1894 to the pediment on the roofline. On the corner of Winchendon Road to the left is the grandly named outlet of the Fulham Cycle and Motor Works where Humber and Raleigh cycles were sold.

Fulham Fire Station, Fulham Road, *c.* 1912. Earl Carrington, chairman of the LCC Fire Brigade Committee, laid the foundation stone on 20 November 1895. The building was refurbished at a cost of several million pounds in 1993 and reopened in March 1994 by Cllr A.G. King JP, chairman of the London Fire & Civil Defence Authority.

Durrell Road, *c.* 1913. The road name was approved as early as 1874 but the planning applications were not served until 1897 for Nos 2 to 8 and in 1898 for 1 to 7.

Epple Road, *c.* 1913. The road name was approved in 1887. The photograph confirms the sequence of drainage applications. In 1889 we have 31 to 45 applied for and in 1890 the Nos 32 to 50 were submitted to the council, followed in 1891 with only 32 and 34. The road was completed in 1898 and 1899. In 1912 we have Arthur E. Philipps, LRCP Lond, MRCS Eng, LSA, physician and surgeon, listed as living at No.50, then still called Herdeswyck.

Landridge Road, *c.* 1913. The road name was approved in 1879. The houses were built upon the site of the former women's prison and in 1912 there are only two properties listed for the east side and thirteen for the west side of the road. The drainage applications for some reason fail to note when the properties were erected but are more than likely to have been built alongside those in neighbouring Fulham Park Gardens in the period 1895 to 1899.

Lilyville Road, *c.* 1914. The road name was approved in 1879. The house drainage applications date from 1887 when only 37 and 39 were submitted. The following years saw only a few houses appear, with the bulk built in 1896 and 1897. Two important trades were mentioned in 1912, that of James Turner at No.5, plumber, and at 47, Walter Poole, decorator.

Munster Road, *c.* 1926. The road name was approved in 1891. On the right, before Bronsart Road, the first shop with the shop blind out is No.259, S. Andrews, florists; at No.257 is Henry Nat Keil & Son, wardrobe dealers; and at No.255 is George Dublin, confectioner. Beyond Bronsart Road at No.253 is Walter Cundell Junior, grocer. The shops have now mainly been converted into small convenience stores and restaurants, although the small newsagents survive.

Munster Road, *c.* 1920. The view is facing north from New Kings Road with St Dionis Road on the right beyond the horse and cart. The plans were submitted to the council for the even-numbered houses on the right, 4 to 20, in 1885 and 1886. The properties on the left, Nos 1 to 23, had plans submitted in 1890 and 1893.

Munster Road, *c.* 1908. In the background, on the corner of Filmer Road, is Munster Road School. The school plans were supplied to the council in 1891 and it was opened on 26 June 1893 and enlarged in 1895. Since March 1997, it has been called St John, Walham Green, C of E Primary School and Nursery. On the corner of Swift Road at 156 Munster Road is John Martin Groessel's bakers and confectionery shop.

Munster Road, *c.* 1920. This section of Munster Road lies between the District Railway Bridge and Fulham Road with Lettice Street on the right. Number 46 Munster Road is the first property on the right and Munster Court flats have been built on the left.

Munster Road School, 1903/4. The playground on the west of Munster Road School is packed out with the girls attending the mixed infant's establishment. The teachers are standing on the steps at the rear. The school was built to accommodate 1,200 pupils.

four

Central Fulham

THE SALISBURY

Lillie Road, *c.* 1914. On the left are Dorset Mansions, dating from 1899, followed by St Clement's Mansions, built about the same time. Bothwell Street is on the left before the second block of St Clement's Mansions and Bishop Creighton House, dating from 1881 at No.378. To the right is the Lillie Road Recreation Ground of 8½ acres. The land, described as the great orchard and gravel pits in the seventeenth century, was bought by Fulham Vestry in 1891 to save it from developers and provide a welcome space in what was becoming a tight suburban network of streets.

Lillie Road, *c.* 1907. St Augustine's church, on the left, started as a mission church in 1884 and services commenced at St Augustine's Mission, 102 Lillie Road, on 6 June 1885. A temporary iron church was in use from September 1886. A mission hall was opened in 1892 that became the parish hall. The church foundation stone was laid on 3 July 1899 and the church, to the designs of architects J.E.K. & J.P. Cutts, was consecrated on 9 October 1900. The church was destroyed by enemy action on 15 October 1940 and the parish hall reverted to use as the main church. It is now partly in use by The Little People of Fulham Montessori day nursery. The church site, on the corner of Moylan Road, was used for housing and flats. On the right is Lillie Road School, opened on 4 September 1891 and enlarged in 1894. The previous temporary school opened here in late 1891. The school was renamed Sir John Lillie Primary School on 1 September 1951.

Fulham Cross, *c.* 1906. The Twynholm building was first intended to become a public house but never gained a licence and was taken in 1893 by the evangelist Sydney Black as a Baptist Mission chapel. The ground floor was let out as coffee and dining rooms as seen here. The title Fulham Cross does not appear in any gazetteer but any local will point out the crossroads of Lillie Road and Munster Road.

Fulham Cross, *c.* 1928. The private motor car was still in its infancy, with most being only small cyclecars, but we see an adventurous motorist making his way between horse-drawn delivery vehicles and the motorised bus as he enters Lillie Road from Munster Road. The Home Stores, on the right, have left out on the pavement their wares for display, and next door is a Loud & Western Laundry receiving office.

Munster Road at the junction with Dawes Road, *c.* 1912. Chaldon Road is to the right. Fulham Cross is at the far end with the Baptist chapel, Twynholm, looming above everything else.

Munster Road, *c.* 1913. On the left at No.320 is Hugo Bass, baker, and at No.318, with the oil jars above his oil shop, is Albert Simmonds, oilman. These stores provided the 1,001 items for the home from candles, brushes, paint, pots and pans to mousetraps and oil for lamps. The third of the premises, at No.316, was the butcher's shop of Robert Harrington, screened from the sunlight to protect the meat on display. On the right is Tucker's provision shop with a pavement display of eggs for sale. On the corner of Strode Road at No.297 is the Fulham Cross Dairy.

Adeney Road *c.* 1909 top and *c.* 1926 lower. The road name was approved in 1881. The house construction here was a long-drawn-out affair with small groups of properties erected from 1882 right up to 1897. A look at the menu and prices at the Fulham Dining Rooms will shock the modern reader, beef steak puddings for 2d or 3d! This and several neighbouring streets were demolished by the Greater London Council in the 1970s to make way for the Bayonne Road Housing Estate.

Bishops Road, *c.* 1914. At No.117, on the corner of Rostrever Road is F. Collins' provision dealer. At 115 are B.T. West's confectioners, the local magnet and attraction for all of these children. This corner has barely changed over the years except for the closure of the shops and conversion of them into private houses.

Bishops Road, *c.* 1914. The road name was approved in 1879. In 1912 the variety of retail outlets included along the right-hand side from 109, Alfred James Brumby, greengrocer, at 107, Matthew Tester, tobacconist and Donald Gunn, oilman at 105 on the corner of Radipole Road, the only shop still trading today as Bishops Food and Wine stores. The cast-iron lamp bracket outside 103, where The Success Stores, wine and spirit stores traded in 1914, has managed to survive. The shop sported an enamel sign for the National Telephone Co. where the public could make their calls. Bloom Park Road is to the left.

Bronsart Road, c. 1908. The road name was approved in 1897. The drainage applications here were submitted in 1892 as for thirty-two houses (not numbered) in 1892, these were probably from 2 to 60 as the numbers from 62 to 144 were submitted in 1899. The house plans on the opposite side were all submitted in 1899.

Burnfoot Avenue, c. 1913. The road name was approved in 1889. The building operations for this road appear to have been completed in small spurts of activity as the house plans were submitted in 1892 for Nos 1 to 15 and 2 to 16 with some small additions up to 20. In 1894 were added the even Nos to 28 and the other side from 25 to 71. Only the two professions were listed in 1912, that of the Snow White Laundry at 74 – this was probably only a receiving house. At 68 was Godfrey Charles McAlester, barrister-at-law.

Dawes Road, c. 1926. The Bedford Arms public house, next to Bedford Passage on the left was built in 1882. The pub has since been rebuilt and renamed the Frog. On the right is the Wilton Arms public house at No.203-205 Dawes Road, built in 1893. The pub was rebuilt in the 1930s but has thankfully retained its original name.

Dawes Road, c. 1914. Here at the corner of Filmar Road in 1912 was the Dawes Road post office at 163, this was also the outlet of James Hare, baker. Following at 161 was J.H. Squires, cheesemonger, and at 159, Charles Briggs, tobacconist. The Salisbury Dairy Co., operated by Alfred H. Sadler was at 157 and on the corner of Salisbury Mews at 155, the coffee rooms of Charles Perkins. One of the Salisbury Mews' two traders was James Clarke, a carman, the modern equivalent would be a delivery driver but in 1912 his transport would amount to a horse and cart. Alongside him operated George Mothersole, farrier. The No.11 bus outside the Salisbury Tavern is en route to Liverpool Street from Shepherds Bush.

Dawes Road, *c.* 1906. The line of shops is named Salisbury Pavement and in 1908 at No.4 was George Savage, pawnbroker, where many household goods such as the best linen would be pawned on a Thursday to feed the family before the wages came in on the following day. The linen would be kept wrapped in the house just for this use. The shop blinds are out above the premises of Ashton & Co., fishmongers at No.5, William Cullen, grocer at No.6, Frank Willis, china and glass dealer at No.7 and at No.8 T.W. Hammett, butcher.

Dawes Road, *c.* 1913. The line of shops here next to Munster Road has the grand title of Royal Parade. In 1912 the outlets included dining rooms and confectionery shops. The taller building at the end of the parade was that of the West London Industrial Co-operative Society Ltd at Nos 243-245. Alongside at No.241 was the West London Co-op Society Ltd bakery. One of the decorative stain-glass roundels of the Co-op survives in the front entrance glass panels of what are today Malcolm Taylor's depositories, storage & removals.

Dawes Road, *c.* 1930. The Salisbury public house was erected in 1887-1888 just as development was in progress along Dawes Road. Sherbrooke Road is to the left and Filmer Road to the right. The pub's name has been altered to The Salisbury Tavern and over the years has lost much of the Victorian architectural decoration on the ground-floor elevation.

Dawes Road, *c.* 1926. The small parade of shops alongside Shorrolds Road, to the left, in 1912 included The Dawes Cycle Works at No.100 and Wilson Brothers, drapers at 98. The Bell telephone sign appropriately appears at the stationers of William Melhuish at 96 and the blinds are covering the goods of Fisher & Son, grocers at 94 and Charles Downs, wardrobe dealers at 92. Squire E. Radcliffe & Partners, Estate Agents occupy 98-100 today (2004).

Mirabel Road, *c.* 1912. The road name was approved in 1886 and development plans laid before the council in the years 1887 to 1891 with the flats at 103 to 149 added in 1892. Only the one trade is listed in 1912, that of C.W. Murfitt, plumber. The early motor car must have proved a rare site in this part of Fulham in 1912. The shopping parade in Dawes Road can be seen in the distance.

Shorrolds Road, *c.* 1914. The road name was approved in 1880 with building operations commencing in 1881 with Nos 8 to 22 planned for the following year. The Fulham Conservative & Unionist Association Club at 2, 4 and 6, near to North End Road, was built in 1884, well before the rest of the houses that were planned to be constructed in 1886 and 1887. In 1912, No.1 was listed as a registered Women's Lodging House with only a James Chapman named.

Strode Road, *c.* 1912. The road name was approved in 1869 with house construction commencing in 1872 and continuing into the 1890s with only two or four properties in any one year completed as shown in the small blocks on the right At the far end is Fulham Cemetery. The houses on the right have largely been demolished together with a few on the left. At No.3 is the off-licence of Richard Pullen, described as a beer retailer in 1912 but the premises has a large gas lamp hanging outside and has the name '★★★pers Arms', possibly Coopers Arms, as a name board and may have operated as a small public house.

St Peter's church, Varna Road, *c.* 1906. The view is from St Peter's Terrace with Varna Road and Bloom Park Road in the background. The church commenced as a mission in December 1879 in a tent. A temporary church was opened in 1881 and services were held here until 1883 when it became the parish hall. It survived until demolition in early 1978 when sheltered housing was built on the site. The foundation stone of the church was laid by the Bishop of London on 4 November 1882 and consecrated on 3 August 1883. The architect of the church was Arthur Billing. A new hall was constructed within the existing church and opened on 29 June 1978.

five

New Kings Road

New Kings Road, *c.* 1925. Cortayne Road is on the right. The corner shop at No.301 is W.E. Botting's fruit and vegetable store which also provided a house and furniture removals service. On the corner of Eddiscombe Road, on the left, with a wonderful display of loaves in the window, is the bakers' of F. Herbert proclaiming his Electric Machine Bakery.

New Kings Road, *c.* 1925. Parsons Green is on the left. The Duke of Cumberland public house, on the corner of Peterborough Road is to the right of the motor car, hidden by the trees. The line of houses, 237 to 245 New Kings Road, to the right of the pub all date from 1795 and bear names such as Albyn, Sefton, Belgrave and Cradley House. On the right is Aragon House, now in use by the Fulham branch of the British Legion.

New Kings Road, *c.* 1925, with Parsons Green to the left and Coniger Road on the right. The parade of shops to the left in 1917 included most of what you would expect to supply the local needs of the residential streets nearby, at No.40, Thomas Wilkey, grocer and telegraphic office, at No.38, Miss Agnes Simpson, fancy draper. At 36 was Dulligall the tobacconist's, 34 was George Ernest Hughes, oilshop, 32- Joseph Hickman, dairy, 30- Charles Templemore, butcher, at 28 was Stephen Nutt- greengrocer and on the corner of Molesford Road at 26 was Arthur Minter, baker.

New Kings Road, *c.* 1925. The small piece of Eelbrook Common to the left has Crondace Road behind. The parade of shops from No.191 downwards, on the right beyond Chiddingstone Road, once providing the daily requirements for the neighbouring households are now estate agents' offices, restaurants and expensive clothes shops.

New Kings Road, *c.* 1926. Eelbrook Common is to the right. The South Fulham Constitutional Club, on the left corner of Chipstead Street was founded here in 1902. The clock above the entrance no longer survives. To the rear, in Chipstead Street is the Kings Hall function rooms of the club. To the west of the club are Kings Hall Mansions and then Quarrendon Street.

New Kings Road, *c.* 1926. The Duke of Cumberland public house, on the corner of Peterborough Road, was built in 1894. The earlier name was the Duke's Head, which remained until renaming in 1971. The name refers to Ernest Augustus, son of George III, who owned much land in the vicinity. A reference from 1657 is given for the Ponds End Tavern that may have stood on this spot.

New Kings Road, *c.* 1906. The larger block on the right is Peterborough Mansions at Nos 65 to 69 New Kings Road. Next along is the Peterborough Hotel, also called the Peterborough Arms. An early reference to the pub is from 1773 but the present building is from the late nineteenth century. The pub has been renamed The Southern Cross. The eighteenth-century line of houses was demolished in the 1930s/1940s for the erection of a three-storey concrete and brick garage and offices numbered 79 to 91. Just four of the houses remain, 71 to 77 next to the mansions.

Lady Margaret School, Parsons Green, *c.* 1926. The Church of England School for Girls was opened in 1917 at Belfield House under the charge of Miss Enid Moberly Bell. Lady Margaret refers to the mother of Henry VII, Lady Margaret Tudor. The school expanded to take in Elm House and Henniker House alongside. The Duke of Clarence (later William IV) kept his mistress Mrs Jordan at Belfield about the year 1785.

Parsons Green, *c.* 1926. The taller building is the White Horse public house, first mentioned in the parish records in 1777 and rebuilt in 1886. Parsons Green is named after the parsonage that stood on the east of the green. Cricket matches were once played here and the green had its own pond that dried out once the main drainage was laid along New Kings Road and had to be filled in.

Parsons Green, *c.* 1926. In 1917 the second house on the left, No.34, was called Holmewood, the dental surgery of Arthur Richard Manning. The first house, No.36, is now called Greenway and 32 was called Flexfield in 1917. In the background is St Dionis church, built in 1885 on the site of the former rectory, dated from 1707 and demolished in 1882 for the church. Parsons Green Mission Hall, on the corner of St Dionis Road, was erected in 1876. The services were held here before the church was built.

Eelbrook Common *c.* 1914 top and *c.* 1926 lower. In the medieval period this was a boggy swamp with streams and ditches crossing the area where tench, carp, roach and eels were still caught in the muddy waters in the 1830s. As late as the eighteenth century the area still posed a problem, requiring infilling of holes and bogs and scouring of ditches. The Ecclesiastical Commissioners in 1878 attempted to sell off some of the common for building land but the locals put up such an argument against that the scheme was abandoned. The common covers fourteen acres.

Ackmar Road, *c.* 1926. The road name was approved in 1880 with planning applications appearing in 1881 for the houses at 2 to 24 consecutive, although building works might not have started in that year. The application for 29 to 34 was not submitted until 1887. At the far end, on the left is the LCC School. The trades listed in 1912 are for the four shops shown in this scene, namely at 2, Joseph Golding, grocer, at No.3– William Livermore, baker, at No.4– J. Pinham, general shop and at No.5– Edward Seaton, dairy.

Alderville Road, *c.* 1914. The road name was approved in 1882 with the first building applications submitted in 1883. In 1912 there were only two trades listed, at No.9 was Samuel Jas Dungate, French polisher and at No.33 Thomas Howes Clarke, carpenter. Neither of these was listed in 1917.

Basuto Road, c. 1926. The road name was approved in 1884 but building applications had been submitted in 1881 and 1882 for all of the properties, including Alex Gossip House, at Nos 2 to 20. This might be a case where the building works had started and on advertising the houses for sale, the road name had to be quickly thought of. The sole trader appears to have been Edward Gudyer, painter at No.37 in 1908.

Bradbourne Road, c. 1926. The road name was approved in 1898 as part of the Peterborough Estate built by the local builder Jimmy Nichols from 1888 onwards. The lions on top of the façade are a feature of these houses on the estate and can be seen in all of the surrounding streets right up to Wandsworth Bridge Road. Planning applications were submitted for the even-numbered houses in 1900 and the odd numbers in 1901. The only person willing to give his profession to the compilers of the local directory in 1917 was Alfred Godtschalk, accountant, a line of work that gives a clue to the type of person the developer was hoping to attract to the estate.

Chiddingstone Road, *c.* 1913. The road name was approved in 1898. Building work must have been a noise and dust nuisance as mountains of brick, cement and timber were transported through Fulham streets for the construction work taking place at the end of the Victorian era in this vicinity. Plans for house construction in Chiddingstone were submitted in 1901, 1902 and 1903.

Chipstead Street, *c.* 1910. The road name was approved in 1898 and all of the house construction plans submitted in 1902. On the right is the Kings Hall to the rear of the South Fulham Constitutional Club on New Kings Road. The two terracotta lions above the hall remain guardians over the roadway.

Coniger Road *c.* 1913 top and *c.* 1926 lower. The road name was approved in 1888, the same year all of the building applications were submitted. In 1912, the Rev. William Parkes Gascoigne, curate of Christchurch, Fulham, lived at No.19. House deliveries are taking place in the earlier scene. The average housewife in those days would rarely be at work and always available at home to receive deliveries from local shops of fresh fish, dairy products and fresh linen and laundry.

Crondace Road, c. 1926. The road name was approved in 1880. The drainage applications were submitted for these three-storey buildings in 1882 and 1883. New Kings Road and the western arm of Eelbrook Common is to the left. In 1917 are listed Thomas Seymour, electrician at No.31 and R.D. Cooper, Insurance Agent at 41. Again it is doubtful if many were willing to give their occupation to compilers of the directories unless it was a means of free advertising for their business carried out in the vicinity.

Delvino Road, c. 1926. The road name was approved in 1880 with some building applications submitted in 1882 and a steady rate of construction up to 1885.

Eddiscombe Road, *c.* 1912. The road name was approved in 1891 when all of the building works were submitted as can be seen by the uniform construction of the houses. In 1912, only William Morris, paperhanger at No.3 gave details of his occupation.

Elmstone Road, *c.* 1912. The road name was approved in 1891 and planning applications for all of the twenty houses were filed the following year.

Elthiron Road, *c.* 1926. The road name was approved in 1880 with planning applications filed in 1882 to 1884. There were no trades listed for this road but in 1912 it was advised that Mrs Bell had apartments to let at No.30. A close inspection of the scene will reveal the number of windows that are open, with the housewives at home and airing the bedrooms.

Favart Road, *c.* 1906. The road name was approved in 1880 with planning applications submitted in 1881 and up to 1885 for these three-storey terraced houses facing Eelbrook Common.

Harbledown Road, *c.* 1913. The road name was approved in 1891 but building work did not commence until 1894 with Nos 1 to 15 and 2 to 18 following in 1896.

Irene Road, *c.* 1926. The road name was approved in 1880 with all of the houses planned to go up in 1883. It would be of interest to find out who Irene was – the builder's wife or daughter perhaps? The plumber Percy Williams was listed in 1917 at No.34.

Linver Road, *c.* 1913. The road name was approved in 1882. The first applications for house construction were filed in 1884 with 1 to 12 inclusive and 25 to 37. A further fifteen properties were filed for in 1885, the majority in 1886 and the last, 26 to 36 in 1887.

Parthenia Road, *c.* 1926. The road name was approved in 1880. The road was built over a long period with the majority of the houses planned for 1881 and 1882 but with the applications for the final four properties, Nos 1, 2, 3 and 4, submitted as late as 1897. In 1912 the one important occupation listed was that of Hugh Kulschitzky, plumber at No.40.

Peterborough School, Clancarty Road, *c.* 1914. The building opened as Peterborough School on 26 August 1901. The school had provision for children with special needs and was to open a classroom for physically disabled children, in the care of specially trained nurse, on 27 November 1905. The school is still called Peterborough Primary School with an age range from three to eleven years and has 190 pupils.

Peterborough Road, *c.* 1913. The road name was approved in 1890. The houses in this scene on the corner of Studdridge Road from 1 to 45 were planned for 1887. To the right is the Hurlingham Club polo ground. The polo ground was compulsory purchased by the LCC after the Second World War and the Sulivan Court housing estate built on the site in the 1950s. The remainder of the land was made a recreation ground named Hurlingham Park and space was also provided for a school.

Rectory Road *c.* 1906 top and *c.* 1914 lower. The road name was given in the 1880s; no exact year was given but it was renamed St Dionus Road in 1938. The house applications were filed in 1883. Prior to the 1880s the road was called Muddy Lane. The rectory for All Saints, Fulham stood facing Parsons Green from 1707 to 1882 when it was demolished for the building of St Dionis church. In 1912, two comparable firms were based alongside each other, at 74 was based Hunt's Hurlingham Laundry and next door at 76, Merryfield & Cracknell, blouse manufacturer. Next to the Mission Hall at No.2 was the Jolly Brewers public house, built in 1894, and next door at No.4, the confectioner's of George Hildersley. The small general store at No.35 grandly named as Guion House was in the charge of Mrs Emily Sharp, listed only as a shopkeeper.

South Park, *c.* 1914. The borough council bought the former nursery lands of the Veitch family in 1903 from Miss Sulivan of Broom House. The park, measuring almost twenty-one acres, was opened in a farcical ceremony in 1904. The Mayor of Fulham had turned up without his mayoral chain as the strongroom key at the town hall had been mislaid. The park caters for cricket, tennis and football and for those who just want to stroll along the walks enjoying the flowerbeds. The park is bounded on the north by Clancarty Road and on the west by Peterborough Road.

Fulham Recreation Ground *c.* 1912 top and *c.* 1906 lower. This land at the corner of Lillie Road and Fulham Palace Road was formerly called Sandell's Corner. The Vestry (precursor of the council) bought the gardener's business there in 1891 as open space among the ever-encroaching streets of housing development. The park of 8½ acres was opened in December 1892. The park contains separate areas laid out for games and children's playground. The ground can appear quite muddy after a winter season of football.

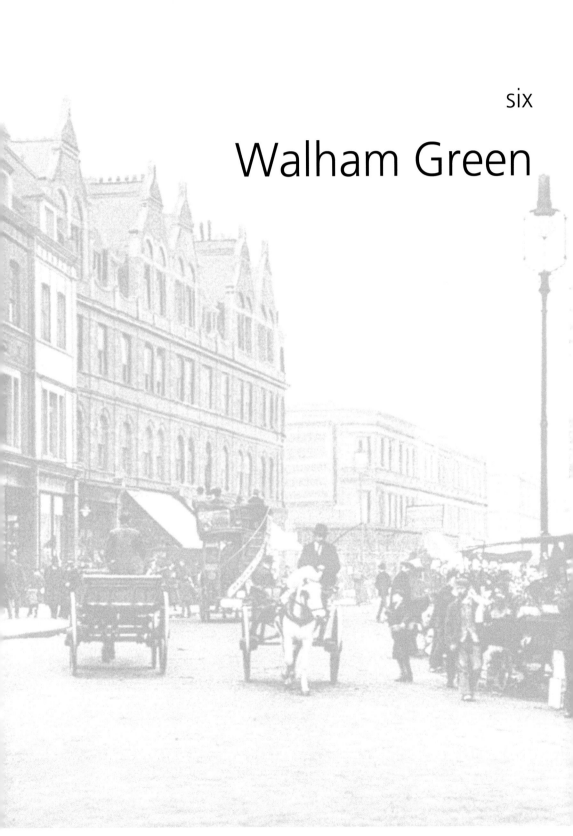

six

Walham Green

The Granville Theatre of Varieties, Walham Green, c. 1914. Dan Leno, the famous music hall comedian, built the theatre. Designed by the theatre architect Frank Matcham, it opened on 19 September 1898 with a capacity of 1,122 seats. The stars appearing there included Marie Lloyd, George Robey and Little Titch. After the Second World War it became a TV studio but was demolished in 1971 after a campaign to save it failed. The beautiful interior was of glazed and majolica tiles. Due to the loss of this fine theatre, the Greater London Council quickly formed a list of threatened theatres across the London area.

The Red Hall cinema, Vanston Place, Walham Green c. 1914. The cinema was designed by Mr George Leslie and opened on 18 December 1913 with seating for 1,600 patrons. The cinema was renamed as the Gaumont Cinema in 1950 and as the Walham Green Gaumont in 1956. It finally closed on 8 December 1962, becoming a bingo hall but survives as the basic frame of a supermarket, the building remaining quite recognisable as in this scene.

The Red Lion public house, 490-492 Fulham Road, Walham Green, *c.* 1908. The pub was first mentioned in the 1770s and has undergone a series of name changes, especially within the last twenty years. It has been called The Golden Lion, Henry J. Beans and now as Havana has been given a garish blue and pink paint scheme although the golden-yellow glazed tiles on the ground floor facade have been cleaned and look splendid.

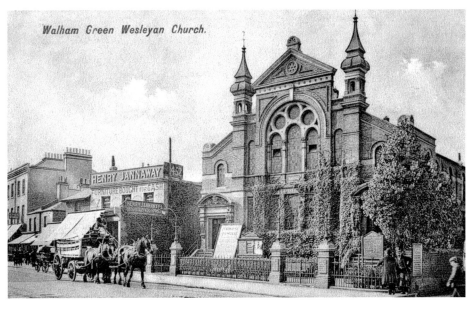

Walham Green Wesleyan Methodist church, *c.* 1906. Services were first held in a small building called Salem chapel about 1811. Services were then held in an iron chapel, opened in November 1882 that remained in use until 1892. The foundation stone for the church, designed by architect Fred Boreham, was laid 1 October 1891 and the church opened on 7 April 1892. The church closed in 1965 and the congregation merged with the Grove Methodist church. The new church was opened in 1971 and was renamed the Fulham Broadway Methodist church.

Walham Green Station top *c.* 1904, bottom *c.* 1913. The station opened in 1880 on the Metropolitan District Railway extension to Putney Bridge from West Brompton. The line was extended to Wimbledon with the construction of the Thames Rail Bridge in 1887-1889. The entrance to Walham Green Station was rebuilt to the designs of H.W. Ford and opened in 1910. Local shopkeepers persuaded London Transport in 1952 to alter the station name to Fulham Broadway, as some visitors were not sure of the location of Walham Green. This is a totally separate entity from Fulham, which lies almost a mile to the south-west. A new development of a supermarket and public house will include a new station entrance almost 100 yards to the east of the old one.

Harwood Road top *c.* 1905, bottom *c.* 1912. The road name was approved in 1863. The town hall was built in 1890 with further extensions added later. F.C. Minter building contractors of Putney are working on the building in the earlier photograph. Effie Road is opposite the town hall. The corner building is today still occupied by a banking concern.

The Broadway, Walham Green, viewed from the corner of Jerdan Place, *c.* 1912. The heart of Walham Green was rebuilt as a modern shopping centre at the end of the nineteenth century, soon after the Metropolitan District Railway opened, but since the Second World War has seen much rebuilding on either side of the road in this scene.

The Broadway, Walham Green, *c.* 1925. Several motor taxis are queuing for fares in the middle of Walham Green, not far from the railway station. The outlets on the left have an array of advertisements on the top parapets of their buildings, the strangest being on Lemmon's Opticians, a pair of staring eyes to greet the passing traveller.

Above: The Broadway, Walham Green, *c.* 1912. The town hall is to the left. The smaller buildings to the left of the White Hart public house were soon to be demolished for an extension to the town hall. A horse-drawn taxicab is resting in the centre of the roadway opposite the station, waiting for fares. The White Hart was first mentioned in the churchwarden's accounts in 1632; an old name for the pub was The Beggar's Rest.

Right: Fulham Town Hall, Walham Green, *c.* 1912. The town hall, erected in 1890, cost £40,000 to construct. A further £20,000 was spent on extending the building to reach through from Fulham Road to Harwood Road. The administrative centre of Fulham from 1890 was relegated to secondary functions when the new borough of Hammersmith and Fulham was formed in 1965 and the town hall in Hammersmith was chosen to serve it.

The Broadway, Walham Green, *c.* 1925. The District Railway station is on the right. The four-storey building in the background is a Barclays Bank. To the right of the bank is the Swan public house, first mentioned in 1769 and rebuilt in the late nineteenth century. The stone swan on the roof has since been removed and the pub has recently been renamed Bootsy Brogan's.

The Broadway, Walham Green, *c.* 1914. The central buildings occupy the site of the former green, once fenced around to keep out any stray animals. In the early eighteenth century Walham Green comprised just a few cottages occupied by market gardeners. The bank building at the centre was built in the Edwardian era and has recently been replaced by a modern office block called, unimaginatively and incorrectly, the Fulham Centre.

Jerdan Place, Walham Green, viewed from the rear of St John's church, *c.* 1913. The former name was The Market Place. The stocks of the village, last used in 1826, were placed just to the south of here. This was the centre of the old village, with a small pond to the north.

North End Road, *c.* 1906. The street market flourished as costermongers were moved from King Street, Hammersmith by local shopkeepers worried about losing trade. The move was to benefit North End Road and the market still attracts large crowds, especially on a Saturday, searching out a bargain on the fruit and vegetable stalls. Many traders today are offering mobile phones, household and cleaning articles, tools and electrical goods.

North End Road, *c.* 1913. The street traders are based on the eastern side of the road, no doubt to benefit from the afternoon sunlight. Epirus Road is on the left and Eustace Road on the right. The block on the right was Frederick Barber's department store. He opened his first draper's shop here in 1891 and over the years the store expanded to take over the entire block from Eustace Road to Armadale Road. The store finally closed in the 1990s.

North End Road, *c.* 1913. Two boys on a donkey cart are making their way among the crowded and frenzied street market. A policeman keeps a wary eye on the multitude from the corner of Anselm Road. Advertisements on the shops advise the passer-by of the offers of cheap unredeemed clothing and linen from a pawnbrokers or the latest drugs, medicines, eyeglasses or teeth from the corner chemists.

Parke's Drug Stores at 316 North End Road, on the corner of Epirus Road, *c.* 1906. Parke's Drug Stores had a chain of pharmacies across most of London before the First World War, supplying a range of products including their own-brand patent medicines. The window display is crammed full of proprietary medicines and camera equipment and materials. The firm specialised in collecting prescriptions and delivering the medicines to your door. The company was eventually taken over by Boots the Chemist.

North End Road, *c.* 1914. The heart of Walham Green village, with Dawes Road on the left and Jerdan Place on the right, seen from North End Road. The centre of the hamlet was a village pond, which had to be filled in due to its stagnant condition in 1814. With an increasing population at the new centre of Fulham, a new church was built on the site of the old pond in 1828 to the designs of J.H. Taylor. The building with the gable end, opposite the church, was Fulham Baths, opened in 1902 and lasting up to 1979 when it closed.

Armadale Road, c. 1913. The road name was approved in 1873. Building plans were submitted in 1877 for Nos 2 to 12 but the properties on the other side of the road were not applied for until 1899 and became part of Barber's drapery shop on North End Road. In 1917 there were two trades at No.9: Oliver Hooper, boot repairer, and William Johnstone, antique dealer. The scene shows a sign above the premises of The International School of Motoring, who also supplied cars for hire.

Dawes Road Congregational church, c. 1906. The church was first founded in Chelsea and moved to Fulham. The first services were held in a lecture hall opened on 16 January 1887. The church opened on 5 April 1887. The church was disbanded at Christmas 1944 after the building had been badly damaged by bombing. The church was largely demolished by the end of 1951 and the site replaced with some small flats called Matthew Court.

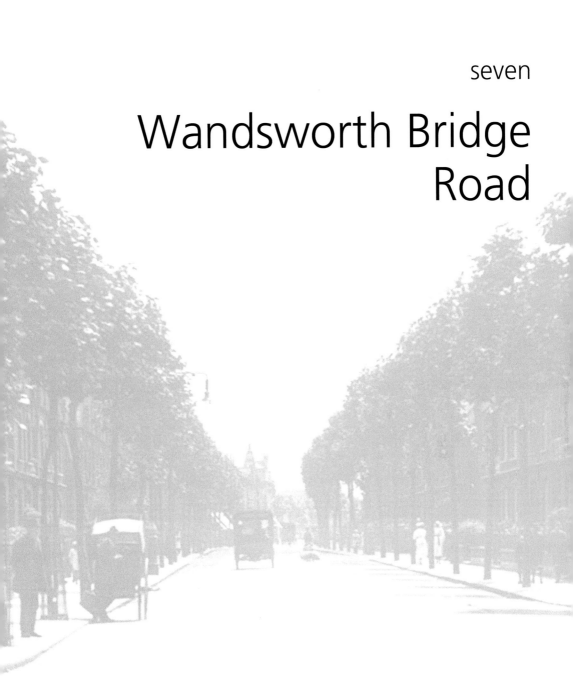

seven

Wandsworth Bridge Road

Wandsworth Bridge top *c.* 1913, bottom *c.* 1906. Designed by Mr J. Tolme, the lattice-girder bridge, on wrought-iron cylinders, had three central spans of 133ft. It was built by the proprietors of the Wandsworth Bridge Co. and opened in 1873 by Colonel Hogg, MP. The bridge was freed of tolls by a ceremony performed by the Prince and Princess of Wales on 26 June 1880. As seen below, the bridge was small and unable to cope with modern traffic. It was replaced in 1938 by the present bridge, which was designed by Mr E.P. Wheeler.

Wandsworth Bridge S. W.

Wandsworth Bridge Road, *c.* 1926. Hugon Road is to the left and Stephendale Road to the right. In 1917 the shops on the right comprised of the following: at 283, Charles Hindle, grocer; at 281 William Godfrey, baker; at 279 William Arthur Weston, dining rooms; and Rees Price, dairyman, at No.275. William Laming repaired boots at 273 and at 271 was the laundry receiving office of Loud & Western Laundry.

Wandsworth Bridge Road, *c.* 1910. A policeman keeps a wary eye out from the corner of Hugon Road for speeding motorists; the term for speeding in the early days of motoring was 'scorching' and woe betide anyone exceeding 12mph. The fencing to the right, next to Rosebury Road, was outside St Matthew's church. The church was built in 1893 and demolished in 1996 and replaced with a smaller building, the rest of the land used for Housing Association flats.

Wandsworth Bridge Road, *c.* 1926. The small shop on the corner of Rosebury Road at No.265 was listed between 1912 and 1917 as Herbert George Rumbold's Italian Stores. Woolneigh Street is to the left.

Wandsworth Bridge Road, *c.* 1913. The only noticeable thing is the nearly empty tree-lined street with only a few boys wandering in the roadway. The houses are identical to those on the rest of the Peterborough Estate.

Wandsworth Bridge Road, top *c.* 1926 and bottom *c.* 1913. South Library is to the left in the upper scene; the photographer is the attraction for many of the children wandering along the pavement. In the lower view, on the right is the Star Kinema on the corner of Broughton Road Approach. The cinema was built in 1913 with seating for 606 patrons. It closed on 4 February 1956 and was eventually demolished in 1961 and has been replaced by a three-storey block of flats with shops at pavement level.

The Wandsworth Road Primitive Methodist chapel, on the corner of Broughton Road Approach and Wandsworth Bridge Road, c. 1926. The church was established in 1871, services being held in premises in Harwood Road and afterwards at 27 Stanley Road, where they were known as the Sotheron Road Society. In September 1888 they moved to Noel Mission Hall. The architect, Revd W. Wray, designed the church whose foundation stone was laid on 1 September 1892. The church opened on 5 February 1893 and closed on 1 January 1967. Hammersmith and Fulham Council acquired the church in 1968 as a health centre. It was demolished in 1970 and sheltered housing built on the site about 1985.

Wandsworth Bridge Road, c. 1925. The display of goods for sale under the awning on the left is at Jn Hancock's Fruiterer at No.120, near the corner of Studdridge Road, and also at the butchers of Hammett Brothers at No.118. The terracotta lions of the Peterborough Estate peer down onto Wandsworth Bridge Road from the pediments of the shopping parade.

Wandsworth Bridge Road, *c.* 1925. It appears that the manager of A. Lyon's corner grocery store at No.99, on the corner of Sandilands Road, is checking the window and fruit display. Every one of the outlets has their blinds out on this west-facing parade on what was a sunny afternoon.

Wandsworth Bridge Road, *c.* 1926. The first outlet on the left next to Clancarty Road is Charles Fraser Collins, pawnbroker, with a large display of second-hand goods on the pavement. The fishmongers of Stephen Dix & Co. traded from No.140 and George Skinner, greengrocer, from No.138. The building at the end of the shopping parade is the South Branch Library, opened in 1896.

Wandsworth Bridge Road, c.1912. This scene of a group of children spread out in a line across the road would be near impossible to recreate in today's world. The only vehicle to gain much speed along the road at the time would have been a motorbike, but the noise would have given adequate warning of his approach and even the buses were limited to 12mph.

Wandsworth Bridge Road, c. 1912. Studdridge Road is on the left. All of the shop windows are packed to the brim with goods on display. The pavements are full of expectant shoppers in this popular trading district. On the corner at 124 is Wills & Sons, oilmen, and next at 126 is John Woodward's Coffee House. Perhaps the reason for the group of children is H.G. Cantelo's confectionery at 128. The hosiery shop at 130 was Oakman & Co., fancy drapers. The canopy on the far side of Studdridge Road covers the bakers shop of H.P. Steel & Son.

Wandsworth Bridge Road, *c.* 1925. The scene facing north along the road, with its young trees, gives an air of a country lane rather than a bustling thoroughfare.

Wandsworth Bridge Road viewed from the corner of New Kings Road, with an early motor bus heading towards Wandsworth Bridge, *c.* 1926. Gapps Ltd, grocers and wine merchants, have their own hand-push cart for deliveries parked outside the premises. The address for the shop is 63 New Kings Road.

Wandsworth Bridge Road, top *c.* 1912 and bottom *c.* 1926. A dutiful father, in the earlier view, wheels a pram with its precious cargo at the corner with New Kings Road. The later scene now has a public toilet in the road junction. The cast-iron stench pipe served an obvious purpose.

Acfold Road, *c.* 1910. The road name was approved in 1890. Only the one person had volunteered any information in 1912; at 36 was Joseph A. Johnson, bootmaker.

Althea Street, *c.* 1926. The road name was approved in 1896. A sign of the times and the need to walk everywhere was that here at No.7 in 1912 was Charles Waite, boot repairer.

Broughton Road, *c.* 1910. The road name was approved in 1888. The directory compilers were only able to persuade four occupants in 1908 to volunteer any information. At 16a lived William Baker, gas fitter; at 22a was a Mrs Maryann Moirat, nurse; an insurance agent, Joseph Thompson, operated from No.90; and James Ward at No.55 was a boot manufacturer.

Beltran Road, *c.* 1926. The road name was approved in 1895 with the house drainage applications all supplied in 1897. In 1912 there were two insurance agents in the road, William Humphreys at No.49 and John Campbell at No.16. Mrs Baker, dressmaker, lived at No.60.

Bowerdean Street, *c.* 1926. The road name was approved in 1893. In 1895, all of the drainage applications were filed at one time on this section of the Peterborough Estate.

Carnwath Cottage, *c.* 1914. These weatherboarded cottages with their own small vegetable garden were once a common site in Fulham, some surviving well into the twentieth century. In the background is Hugon Road School.

De Morgan Road, *c.* 1914. The road name was approved in 1888 but the drainage applications were not submitted until 1896. The local directory for 1912 only lists the names of four occupants, the rest had either refused to volunteer any information or were too busy in employment in this working-class district. At the far end, in Townmead Road, is the Van der Bergh margarine factory. The De Morgan tile factory was founded in Townmead Road in 1888. The Bluebell Polish factory occupied the large building on the far corner of De Morgan Road. After closing, the factory was demolished and the site used for the local authority Townmead housing estate, built in 1964.

Hamble Street, *c.* 1914. The road name was approved in 1896 with all of the drainage applications supplied in 1897. Similar to De Morgan Road, only four occupants volunteered any information to the directories, two with their names only and a Mrs Rose, dressmaker at 29 and Joseph Ernest Banks, insurance agent, at 41.

Hazelbury Road, *c.* 1914. No date is given for the submission or approval of the road name but the drainage applications were submitted in 1889 and 1890. The road forms part of the Hever Estate and here gives the appearance of a playground with the amount of children in the street. Isaac Wilson advertised flats for sale at their estate agents office. Harry Arthur Lockington ran the grocery store and post office at No.1 and only a few residents gave any information to the directory compilers. Arthur Shaw-Mackenzie, physician and surgeon, had his surgery at 37; Miss M.J. Luck made her dresses at 131, and George M. Codd at 143 collected money as an insurance agent.

Hugon Road, *c.* 1914. The road name was approved in 1878. The house drainage schemes were submitted in 1881, 1885 and 1887. Hugon Road School was built in 1893. At the far end can be seen the factory of the Drayton Paper Works in Peterborough Road. The firm was established here about 1850 and remained until 1988.

Rosebury Road, *c.* 1914. No date is given for the approval of the road name but as part of the Hever Estate it would have been put forward in the 1880s. House drainage applications were filed in 1889 for all of the properties. The spire of St Matthew's church on Wandsworth Bridge Road can be seen at the far end.

Rycroft Street, *c.* 1914. The road name was approved in 1893. The house drainage applications were submitted in 1895 for all of the units.

Sandilands Road, *c.* 1912. No date is given for the acceptance or approval of the road name. Applications for connection to the main drainage for the houses were mainly filed in 1884 and 1886. At the far end of the road are the gasholders of Fulham Gasworks.

Settrington Street, *c.* 1912. The road name was approved in 1895. A complication rears its head as to when the houses in this street were built, as the only drainage applications to survive are for Nos 36 to 108, dated 1899. George Wilson, builder, at No.48, was the only person to give his occupation in 1912.

Stephendale Road, *c.* 1914. The road name was approved in 1878. The majority of the house applications were supplied in 1896 and 1897, although some had been filed in 1884, 1886 and 1889.

Above and below: Stephendale Road, *c.* 1914. The uniform nature of these houses would put them into the somewhat later phase of development, either in 1889 or the period 1896-1897.

Studdridge Street, *c.* 1912. The road name was approved in 1888. The house drainage plans were filed with the council in 1896 for Nos 1 to 31 and in 1899 for 33 to 43.

Christ Church, Studdridge Street, *c.* 1909. Services were first held in a room of Peterborough House during 1900 and 1901 and then in a hall at Peterborough Road School from 1 November 1901 until the church was ready. The architects of the church were J.E.K. & J.P. Cutts. The foundation stone was laid on 18 October 1902 and it was consecrated on 24 January 1909. The foundation stone for the hall was laid on 19 May 1903 and it was opened on 26 November 1903. A new hall was constructed within the existing church and opened on 12 October 1991.

eight

Around & About

Broomhouse Road, *c.* 1914. Broomhouse was a small hamlet near the riverside first recorded in the fifteenth century. It takes its name from broom plants, a yellow-flowering bush that grows on sandy soils whose twigs and branches were taken for use as brushes to sweep floors.

Broomhouse Road, *c.* 1906. On the left are the grounds of Broom House, later taken over by the Hurlingham Club as their polo ground. On the right is the entrance to Wilson's Cottage and in the distance the tower of The Elizabethan School. The condition of the gravel-surfaced lane was not improved until 1963 when the borough council adopted it and built pavements on either side with a tarmac roadway.

The Elizabethan School, Broomhouse Road, *c.* 1912. The school was built in 1855 as a ragged charity school (for children too poor, hence ragged, for any other type of school) with two almshouses attached, by the Hon. Laurence Sulivan of Broom House, which stood on the other side of Broomhouse Lane. The school was constructed in memory of his wife, Elizabeth, sister of Lord Palmerston, the famous Prime Minister, hence the Elizabethan style and name for the school. The school, purchased by the LCC in 1904 and now used by the borough council's education department, has a preservation order on it.

Broomhouse, c. 1895. This elegant house was probably built about 1763 when several ladies had possession of the eight-acre estate. The Sulivan family bought the house in 1823 and proved great benefactors to the local populace, selling land at a low rate for the building of South Library and several local churches. Mrs Sulivan was sister to Lord Palmerston and he often visited the house; it is said he planned the Crimean War during his visits here. The Sulivan Court Council Estate, built in the 1950s, was named after the family. The house and grounds were bought by the Hurlingham Club in 1911 and demolished in 1912.

Broomhouse Road, c. 1914. The houses in this section of the road just to the south of New Kings Road were planned for construction between 1885 and 1887.

Above and below: Hurlingham Club and grounds, *c.* 1906. The house was built about 1800 but the central part dates back to 1760 when it was erected for Dr Cadogan, an eminent physician. Famous residents included the Marquis Wellesley, brother to the Duke of Wellington, and several Governors of the Bank of England. In 1869 it became the Hurlingham Club, a pigeon-shooting club. Other sports included tennis, croquet, archery and golf but the club became a fashionable venue with their first polo match in 1874.

Hurlingham Club grounds, above, and smoking lounge, below, *c.* 1906. The polo grounds were extended with the purchase of Mulgrave House and its fifteen acres in 1879 and also of Broom House and its eight acres in 1911, both properties being demolished by the club. The land was compulsorily purchased by the LCC after the Second World War, with Sulivan Court housing estate built on polo ground number two and Hurlingham Park created on polo ground number one, leaving the club with forty-two acres.

Above and below: Hurlingham, *c.* 1906. In 1908 a mile-long gas main was laid especially from the gasworks at Imperial Road for the balloon flights organised by the Royal Aero Club. These took place here up to 1912. Firework displays would accompany the balls and receptions held here. Long lines of carriages down Broomhouse Lane could be seen before the First World War awaiting entrance to the grounds, and local children were enthralled by the elegant ladies, top-hatted gentlemen and their attendant servants. The club built an outdoor swimming pool in 1933, a squash court in 1934 and bowls were introduced in 1935. The club has 10,000 members today.

West Kensington underground railway station, *c.* 1914. The District Railway Co. extended their line to Hammersmith on 9 September 1874, opening this station as North End Station. It was renamed as West Kensington Station in 1877, lasting only three years as North End. To the left is the Three Kings public house.

Barons Court underground railway station, Palliser Road, *c.* 1914. The station opened in 1905 as the Great Northern, Piccadilly & Brompton railway line was extended to Hammersmith. The American entrepreneur Charles Tyson Yerkes planned the railway. He had acquired the District Railway Co. in 1901 to fund construction of lines from Baker Street to Hampstead and Waterloo and the Great Northern, Piccadilly & Brompton railway but died in 1905 before the lines were completed.

Seagrave Hospital, *c.* 1914. The hospital was established in 1877 as the Fulham Smallpox Hospital, later called the Western Fever Hospital when it catered for other infectious diseases. The hospital was enlarged in 1896–1898. The hospital specialised in chest complaints and geriatrics during its last years and closed in the late 1970s/early 1980s. A private residential estate of 300 units called Brompton Park Crescent was built on the site between 1984 and 1986.

Margravine Gardens, *c.* 1914. The road name was approved in 1894. The house drainage applications were submitted in 1884 for No.5 and in 1890 for six properties at 2 to 12. The rest of the properties were planned for the period 1894 to 1897.

Other local titles published by The History Press

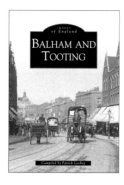

Balham and Tooting
PATRICK LOOBEY

In this intriguing collection of old postcards and photographs, the Balham and Tooting of the past has been thoughtfully recreated. This book provides the reader with the opportunity to witness the vibrant history of an ever-changing inner London area.
0 7524 2203 0

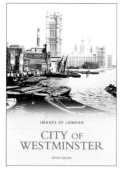

City of Westminster
BRIAN GIRLING

This stunning collection of old photographs of one of Britain's best-known areas will fascinate all who embark on this short tour into the Edwardian period of London's old City of Westminster.
0 7524 3191 9

London – Life In The Post-War Years
DOUGLAS WHITWORTH

These superb photographs show the extent of Blitz damage to famous streets and buildings, even in the very heart of the city, and illustrate how London looked, in its parks, streets and shops, as life began to get back to normal.
0 7524 2816 0

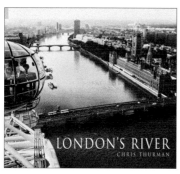

London's River – Westminster to Woolwich
CHRIS THURMAN

These photographs of the Thames capture the changes that have taken place along its banks, from the decline of shipping to the demolition of warehouses and the expansion of housing along the banks. *London's River – Westminster to Woolwich* captures the changing face of the Thames as it runs through central London.
0 7524 2595 1

If you are interested in purchasing other books published by The History Press, or in case you have difficulty finding any of our books in your local bookshop, you can also place orders directly through our website
www.thehistorypress.co.uk